A Faith to Live By

Selected Writings from
Sixteenth-Century Anabaptists

J. C. WENGER

HERALD PRESS
Scottdale, Pennsylvania
Kitchener, Ontario

A FAITH TO LIVE BY
Copyright © 1980 by Mennonite Board of Missions,
   Elkhart, Ind. 46514
Published by Herald Press,, Scottdale, Pa. 15683
   Released simultaneously in Canada by Herald Press,
   Kitchener, Ont. N2G 4M5
Library of Congress Catalog Card Number: 79-89441
International Standard Book Number: 0-8361-1909-6
Printed in the United States of America
Illustrations and cover art by Elmore Byler
Design: Alice B. Shetler

15 14 13 12 11 10 9 8 7 6 5 4 3 2 1

Distributed overseas by Media Ministries,
Box 1252, Harrisonburg, Va. 22801

CONTENTS

PREFACE

Followers of Jesus can be found today all over the world. Among these Christians are Mennonites who take their name from Menno Simons, a Frisian Reformer of the sixteenth century.

Until the nineteenth century, most Mennonites were found in Europe and North America. However, mission, relief, and service activities during the twentieth century have resulted in a worldwide Mennonite fellowship.

One major emphasis of the Mennonites is to practice daily the teachings of Jesus as found in the Bible. This book sets forth some of these teachings concerning the Word of God, as expressed by leading Anabaptists of the sixteenth century.

J.C. Wenger, a lifelong student and teacher of Anabaptism, has selected brief statements that highlight biblical truths. The quotes, along with the chapter titles and lead sentences, point the way to a rewarding life today.

A Faith to Live By is volume nine of the Mennonite Faith Series listed inside the back cover. The references placed at the back of this book will assist anyone wanting to read and understand more of the writings of the Anabaptists.

Mennonite Board of Missions, Elkhart, Indiana, commissioned the Mennonite Faith Series to help bridge the gap between scholarly Mennonite writing and non-Mennonite literature that emphasizes salvation, but often neglects discipleship.

J. Allen Brubaker

THE KEY TO
SELF-UNDERSTANDING

Read and believe the Word of God. "O dear Lord, I did not know myself until I viewed myself in Thy Word. And then I confessed my nakedness and blindness, my sickness, my native depravity, and with Paul I realized that in my flesh dwelt no good thing. . . . My thoughts were carnal, my words and works without the fear of God. My waking and sleeping were unclean, my prayer hypocrisy. Nothing I did was done without sin. O Lord, remember not the sins of my youth, committed knowingly and unknowingly so oft before Thee, nor my daily transgressions in which because of my great weakness I am alas

5

found daily, but remember me according to Thy great mercy."

—Menno Simons, *Complete Writings,* 70

"Thus did I, miserable sinner, spend my days and did not, O God of grace, acknowledge Thee as my God, Creator, and Redeemer, till Thy Holy Spirit taught me through Thy Word and made known to me Thy will, and led me somewhat into Thy mysteries. Now I know how dishonorably I walked before Thee, not otherwise than if I had spit in Thy face, had struck Thee with the hand, and trampled Thee and derided Thee as foolish."

—Menno, *CW,* 77

Respond to God's gracious work in you. "Dearly beloved, since you find within you the beginning of the work of the eternal invincible God, which has almost imprisoned your heart and is intent on driving you away from the self-seeking of carnal life ... give heed ... not to cast [His work] into the wind nor let it pass over your heads. ..."

—Hans Denck, *Writings,* 76

God changes our sinful nature when we yield to Him. "Sovereign Lord, Lord of heaven and earth, I call Thee Lord, though I am not worthy to be called Thy servant; for from my youth I served not Thee, but Thine enemy the devil with diligence. And yet I do not doubt Thy graciousness, for I find in the word of Thy truth that Thou art a bountiful Lord unto all those who call upon Thee. Therefore I call unto Thee, O Lord, hear me; hear me, O Lord!"

—Menno, *CW*, 66

"Although I resisted in former times Thy precious Word and Thy holy will with all my powers, and with full understanding contended against Thy manifest truth, taught and lived and sought my own flesh, praise, and honor, more than Thy righteousness, honor, word, and truth; nevertheless Thy fatherly grace did not forsake me, a miserable sinner, but in love received me, converted me to another mind, led me with the right hand ... [you] taught me by the Holy Spirit until of my own choice I declared war upon the world, the flesh, and the devil, and renounced all my ease, peace, glory, desire, and physical prosperity ... [you taught me until I] willingly submitted to the heavy cross of my Lord Jesus Christ that I might inherit the promised kingdom with all the soldiers of God and the disciples of Christ."

—Menno, *CW*, 69

Children are saved until they can understand their need of a Savior. "We hold that all children who have not yet come to the discernment of the knowledge of good and evil, and who have not yet eaten of the tree of knowledge, are certainly saved through the suffering of Christ."

—Conrad Grebel, *Programmatic Letters*, 226

Four kinds of sin: "The Scriptures as I see

[them] speak of different kinds of sin. The first kind is the corrupt, sinful nature, namely, the lust or desire of our flesh contrary to God's Law ... sin which is inherited at birth ... and is not inaptly called original sin. ... Now for Christ's sake, it is not counted as sin unto us. Romans 8:5-8.

"The second kind of sins are the fruits of this first sin and are not inaptly called actual sin by theologians. ... Adultery, fornication, avarice, dissipation, drunkenness, hatred, envy, lying, theft, murder, and idolatry. ... [These result] in God's wrath and [in] death, unless these sins are repented of. ...

"The third kind of sins are human frailties, errors, and stumblings which are still found daily among saints and regenerate ones, such as careless thoughts, careless words, and unpremeditated lapses in conduct. ... There is this difference. The unbelieving ... as yet unchanged ... commit sin with relish and boldness ... But those who are born from above are fearful of all sin. ... Therefore they fight daily with their weak flesh in the Spirit and in faith. ... They approach the throne of grace daily with contrite hearts. ...

"The fourth kind of sin is this. After one is enlightened ... [if he] rejects the Spirit and Word of God ... hates and blasphemes and reviles all truth ... ascribing it to the devil— notwithstanding his conscience convinces him that it is the ... work of God; and he then returns to the broad way, and says ... I refuse to be subjected. ...

"In such a case let ... [the members of the

church] admonish such a one according to the Word of the Lord. If he repents heartily, if he shows true fruits of repentance . . . if he receives a broken, contrite, and penitent heart . . . then it is manifest that he did not sin against the Holy Spirit. But if he remains impenitent . . . his end and reward will be death."

—Menno, *CW*, 563-5

The low moral condition of the world: "And how wickedly you poor ignorant people live, and how far you are from the innocence of children. . . . For you despise God and His Word; you hate all righteousness and truth; many of you live as the irrational creatures; others go to law, and fight, curse, swear, rake, scrape, practice usury, lie, cheat, hurt, and defraud one another. . . . It is gambling, gaming, drinking, and carousing."

—Menno, *CW*, 213

2

GOOD NEWS FOR
TROUBLED HEARTS

Christ takes our sins away. "O Lord, dear Lord, have mercy upon me, for I am desolate and afflicted; my sins are many and great; my conscience troubles me; my thoughts disturb me; my heart laments and sighs because I have sinned so heinously before Thee. . . . And yet the deeper I am grieved, the more I am consoled by Thy Word, for it teaches me Thy mercy, grace, and favor and the remission of my sins through Christ, Thy beloved Son, our Lord, ignoring the fact that I neither knew nor feared Thee. This promise quiets me. This promise gladdens me; it leads me with the sinful woman to Thy blessed feet with full confidence and clear conscience, knowing that Thou didst not reject Thy returning son although I have spent my paternal inheritance dishonorably ... in a strange country. ..."   —Menno, *CW*, 77, 78

Christ's mission as Redeemer (as Christ might have said it). "By the kindness of my heavenly Father, I am come into the world, and by the power of the Holy Spirit, I became a visible, tangible, and dying man; in all points like unto you, sin excepted. I was born of Mary, the unpolluted mother and pure virgin; I descended from heaven, sprang from the mouth of the Most High, the first-born of every creature, the first and last, the beginning and the end, the Son of the Almighty God; anointed with the Holy Spirit to preach the Gospel to the poor, to bind up the brokenhearted, to proclaim liberty to the captives, to give sight to the blind, to open the prison to them that are bound, and to proclaim the acceptable year of the Lord. ... I am the Lamb that was sacrificed for you. I take away the sins of the whole world. My Father has made me unto you wisdom, righteousness, sanctification, and redemption. ... Yea, all that believe that I am He, shall have eternal life."
   —Menno, *CW*, 115, 116

" ... I left the glory of my Father, and came into this sad world as a poor slave to serve you. For I saw that you all belonged to the devil, and that there was none to redeem you..... Therefore did I come from heaven, and became a poor, weak, and dying man, in all things like unto you, sin excepted. In my great love I sought you out with zeal, found you miserable, sorrowful, yes, half dead. The services of my love I have demonstrated so heartily toward you; your sores I bandaged; your blood I wiped away; wine and oil I have poured into your putrid wounds ... the law I have fulfilled for you; your sins I took away."   —Menno, *CW*, 147

"Through His suffering Christ has made satisfaction for the sin of all men."
                          —Hans Denck, *Writings*, 124

Christ, the center of the good news: "That Gospel is the blessed announcement of the favor and grace of God to us, and of forgiveness of sins through Christ Jesus. Faith accepts this Gospel through the Holy Spirit, and does not consider former righteousness or unrighteousness, but hopes against hope (Rom. 4:18), and with the whole heart casts itself upon the grace, Word, and promises of the Lord, since it knows that God is true, and that His promises cannot fail. In this the heart is renewed, converted, justified, becomes pious, peaceable, and joyous, is born a child of God, approaches with full confidence the throne of grace, and so becomes a joint heir of Christ and a possessor of eternal life."
                          —Menno, *CW*, 115

Steps in becoming a believer. "Those who become Christians awaken in time. They hear and believe the Word of the Lord. They weep over

their past vain lives and conduct. They desire help and aid for their sick souls. To such, Christ who is a comforter for all troubled hearts says, Believe the Gospel, that is, fear not; rejoice and be comforted; I will not punish nor chastise you, but will heal you, comfort you, and give you life. A bruised reed will I not break, and smoking flax will I not quench. . . . I am not come to call the righteous, but sinners to repentance."
—Menno, *CW*, 115

Faith lays hold on all God's good gifts: " . . . Faith in Christ Jesus . . . effects repentance, salvation . . . justification and purification . . . sanctification, the forgiveness of sins . . . and eternal life. . . . This faith is the means whereby we . . . receive the promised Spirit, whereby we are God's children, and whereby Christ lives in our hearts." —Pilgram Marpeck, *Writings*, 89

God's love moves His children to serve: "God does not force anyone to remain in His service who is not compelled by love."
—Hans Denck, *Writings*, 126

The Holy Spirit gives penitent believers a new nature: "The new birth consists, verily, not in water nor in words; but it is the heavenly, living, and quickening power of God in our hearts which flows forth from God, and which by the preaching of the divine Word, if we accept it by faith, quickens, renews, pierces, and converts our hearts, so that we are changed and converted from unbelief to faith, from unrighteousness to

13

righteousness, from evil to good, from carnality
to spirituality, from the earthly to the heavenly,
from the wicked nature of Adam to the good nature of Jesus Christ."
—Menno, *CW*, 265

" . . . We must confess that we cannot be led to
this godly gift of faith and regeneration otherwise
than by the Word of God through His Holy
Spirit."   —Menno, *CW*, 271

The Spirit seals the Word in our hearts: " . . .
At Pentecost, in the presence of many people,
external noise, wind, and strange tongues were
His witness . . . to His promise. This testimony is
contained in the writings of the New Testament.
He who has this Scripture sealed in his heart, this
common Spirit of salvation, he alone, and no one
else, can bear testimony to it. This Spirit of
promise and clarity from God is here and now in
the elect an open indicator, foretaste, seal, and
down payment of future glory. . . ."
—Pilgram Marpeck, *Writings*, 64

Christians are saved by God's grace in Christ:
"Think not . . . that we boast of being perfect
and without sins. Not at all. . . . If God should
judge us according to our deserts and not according to His great goodness and mercy, then I
confess with the holy David that no man could
stand before His judgment. Ps. 143:2. Therefore,
it should be far from us that we should comfort
ourselves with anything but the grace of God
through Christ Jesus. For He it is and He alone

14

and none other who has perfectly fulfilled the righteousness required of God. ... All saints from the beginning have lamented the corruption of their flesh. ..."

—Menno, *CW*, 506

3

GOD IS TRIUNE

One eternal true God: Father, Son, and Holy Spirit: " ... I have been diligent, with great heaviness in my poor sick body, to send you my inmost faith and confession concerning the eternal Triune God, Father, Son, and Holy Spirit, derived from the pure Word of God. ...

"This one and only eternal, omnipotent, incomprehensible, invisible, ineffable, and indescribable God, we believe and confess with the Scriptures to be the eternal, incomprehensible Father, with His eternal, incomprehensible Son, and with His eternal incomprehensible Holy Spirit. The Father we believe and confess to be a true Father, the Son a true Son, and the Holy Spirit a true Holy Spirit. . . . We also believe and confess the eternal begetting heavenly Father, and the eternally begotten Son, Christ Jesus. . . . We believe and confess the Holy Spirit to be a true, real, and personal Holy Spirit . . . and that in a divine fashion, even as the Father is a true Father and the Son a true Son. . . .

"And so we believe and confess before God, before His angels, before all our brethren, and before all the world, that these three names, activities, and powers, namely, the Father, the Son, and the Holy Spirit (which the fathers called three persons, by which they meant the three, true, divine beings) are one incomprehensible, indescribable, Almighty, holy, eternal, and sovereign God. . . .

" . . . I confess that I would rather die than to believe and teach my brethren a single word or letter concerning the Father, the Son, and the Holy Spirit (before God I lie not) contrary to the plain testimony of the Word of God. . . ."

—Menno, *CW*, 490, 491, 495-497

4

CHRIST'S DISCIPLES, THE CHURCH, ENJOY HIS BLESSINGS

The rewarding life of true Christians: "These regenerated people have a spiritual king over them who rules them by the unbroken scepter of His mouth, namely, with His Holy Spirit and Word. He clothes them with the garment of righteousness. ... He refreshes them with the living water of His Holy Spirit, and feeds them with the Bread of Life. His name is Christ Jesus.

"They are the children of peace who have beaten their swords into plowshares and their spears into pruning hooks, and know war no more. They give to Caesar the things that are Caesar's and to God the things that are God's.

"Their sword is the sword of the Spirit, which they wield in a good conscience through the Holy Spirit.

"Their marriage is that of one man and one woman, according to God's own ordinance.

"Their kingdom is the kingdom of grace, here in hope and after this in eternal life.

"Their citizenship is in heaven, and they use the lower creations such as eating, drinking, clothing, and shelter, with thanksgiving and to the necessary support of their own lives, and to the free service of their neighbor, according to the Word of the Lord.

"Their doctrine is the unadulterated Word of God, testified through Moses and the prophets, through Christ and the apostles, upon which they build their faith, which saves their souls. . . .

"Their baptism they administer to the believing according to the commandment of the Lord, and according to the doctrine and practice of the apostles.

"Their Lord's Supper they celebrate as a memorial of the favors and death of their Lord, and an incitement to brotherly love.

"Their ban or excommunication descends on all the proud scorners—great and small, rich and poor, without any respect of persons, who once passed under the Word but have now fallen back, those living or teaching offensively in the house of the Lord—until they repent."
—Menno, *CW*, 94

The disciple of Christ receives eternal life: "We teach and direct you in the right way which

you should walk if you wish to be saved. We do not point you to the pope, or to Luther, or Augustine, or Jerome, but with the Scriptures to Christ Jesus: to hear Him, to believe and faithfully follow Him. For He is the Prophet promised of God, the Teacher sent of God, the Light of the world, the true Shepherd of our souls. Whoever shall hear, believe, and follow Him has eternal life. He calls to emperor, king, and common man, Except ye be converted, and become as little children, ye shall not enter into the kingdom of heaven. If any man will come after me (or whoever will be a true Christian), let him deny himself, and take up his cross, and follow me. Whoever loves anything more than me cannot be my disciple, and is not worthy of me."
—Menno, *CW*, 553

The church emphasizes faithfulness, not numbers: "It is far preferable that a few be rightly instructed in the Word of God, believing aright, walking in virtues, and observing [biblical] rites than that many through adulterated doctrine falsely and deceitfully 'believe.' "
—Conrad Grebel, *Programmatic Letters*, 25

Building the church—a goal worth living for: ". . . to preach the Gospel, make disciples by means of the doctrine, baptize these same disciples, and so gather unto the Lord a peculiar people, who should walk in Christ Jesus in righteousness, truth, and obedience, as the regenerate children of God, and thank His great and glorious name forever. And with such a people that walks in His fear, love, Word, ordinances, and commands, He will always be, even to the end of the world."

—Menno, *CW*, 701

Rich reward is found by returning to Christ's teachings: "God's holy Word which was obscured for such a long time has through our little talent been brought back to light."

—Menno, *CW*, 105

"... Although it is so little regarded ... yet this book of Christ, by the grace of God, has been found again by some. The pure, unfalsified truth has come to light through the pure, undiluted Gospel, and is plainly read in your ears; it is expounded before your eyes with a godly virtuous life, with confident confession, and with much of the property and blood of the saints. ..."

—Menno, *CW*, 361

"In these latter days the gracious, great God by the rich treasures of His love has again opened the windows of heaven and let drop the dew of His divine Word, so that the earth once more as of yore produces its green branches and plants of righteousness which bear fruit unto the Lord and glorify His great and adorable name. The holy Word and sacraments of the Lord rise up again from the ashes. ..."

—Menno, *CW*, 502, 503

"... The most merciful God and Father,

through His unfathomable grace and goodness, has again in these last days of unbelief and abominations, of sin and idolatries ... set forth before the eyes and consciences of some, His blessed, His holy, and eternal Son Jesus Christ, who was unknown for so many centuries. He has once more opened the book ... of eternal truth, the book which had been closed for so many centuries. ..."

—Menno, *CW*, 581

Pastors set an example: "The shepherd in the church shall be a person, according to the rule of Paul, fully and completely, who has a good report of those who are outside the faith. The office of such a person shall be to read and exhort and teach, warn, admonish, discipline or ban in the congregation, and properly to preside among the sisters and brothers in prayer and in the breaking of bread, and in all things to take care of the body of Christ, that it may be built up and developed, so that the name of God might be praised and honored. ..."

—*Schleitheim Confession*, 13

Pastors need the support of the church: The pastor "shall be supported, wherein he has need, by the congregation which has chosen him, so that he who serves the gospel can also live therefrom, as the Lord has ordered."

—*Schleitheim Confession*, 13

"... Pastor diligently, preach and teach valiantly, cast from you all filthy lucre ... rent a farm, milk cows, learn a trade if possible, do manual labor as did Paul, and all that which you then fall short of will doubtlessly be given and provided you by pious brethren ... as necessity requires."   —Menno, *CW*, 451

"Be liberal towards all that are in want among you ... but especially toward those who labor among you in the Word, and are driven about, and cannot eat their bread in peace and quietness."   —Michael Sattler, *Martyrs Mirror*, 420

True faith centers in Christ: "O Lord, I am not ashamed of my doctrine before Thee and Thine angels, much less before this rebellious world, for I know assuredly that I teach Thy Word. I have taught nothing all along but true repentance, a dying unto our sinful flesh, and the new life that comes from God. I have taught a true and genuine faith in Thee and Thy beloved Son; that it must be active through love. I have taught Jesus Christ and Him crucified, true God and man, who in an incomprehensible manner was born of Thee before all time, Thy eternal Word and Wisdom, the brightness of Thy glory and the express image of Thy person; and that in fullness of time through the power of Thy Holy Spirit He became, in the womb of the unspotted Virgin Mary, real flesh and blood; a visible, tangible, and mortal man, like unto Adam and his posterity in all things, sin excepted; born of the seed or lineage of Abraham and David; that He died and was buried, arose again, ascended into

heaven and so became our only and eternal Advocate before Thee; our Mediator, Intercessor, and Redeemer. ... I have taught no other baptism, no other supper, no other ordinance than that implied by the unerring mouth of our Lord Jesus Christ, and the manifest example and practice of His holy apostles. ..."
—Menno, *CW*, 80, 81

Conversion is primary, ordinances secondary: "... Do not imagine that we put great stress upon elements and rites. ... If anyone were to come to me, even the emperor or the king, desiring to be baptized, but walking still in the ... lusts of the flesh, and the ... regenerated life were not in evidence ... I would rather die than baptize such an impenitent carnal person."
—Menno, *CW*, 139

God's concern is to pour His love into our hearts: "Love is the total content of Scripture." [More literally, "All which the Scripture teaches us and sets forth is love."]
—Menno, *CW*, 917

"The more one resists this consuming fire [of God's desire for us to be one with Him], the more unrest it causes. ... The more ... [a person] gives up his own ... [will], the sooner God is able to reach His goal."
—Hans Denck, *Writings*, 87

"O you who thirst after Love, seek Love while she may be found, for God the Lord offers her

24

free of charge to all who desire her with their hearts. . . ."

—Hans Denck, *Writings*, 118, 119

"Love is the sum of the Law and no one can too highly regard or understand it or carry it out. He who daily improves in Love, does not thereby add anything to the Law, but simply fulfills it. Love consists in this, to know God and love Him and to learn to lose for His sake and hand over to the Lord all creatures which may be pleasing to man in the flesh. . . ."

—Hans Denck, *Writings*, 108

5

THE GREAT ORDINANCES
OF CHRIST'S CHURCH
AFFIRM FAITH

Christ established meaningful ordinances to enrich His church: "If God would have His ceremonies under the law—which were in part attended with trouble, and difficult and quite numerous, and which He commanded not through Christ, His Son, but through His servant Moses—if God wanted these ceremonies kept thus strictly and unchanged until the time of Christ; how much more so does He want the few ceremonies, but two in number, of the New Testament kept strictly and unchanged: [namely,] baptism and the Supper, which He commanded not through His servant [Moses] but through His only begotten Son, Jesus Christ; and which are neither attended with trouble nor difficulty."　　　　—Menno, *CW*, 237, 238

Baptism

Baptism with water expresses faith in Christ: "In this manner Christ has commanded baptism and received it Himself. . . . He prepared Himself to meet temptation, misery, the cross, and death, and as a willing, obedient child resigned Himself to the will of His almighty Father—as He Himself said that He came down from heaven, not to do His own will, but the will of Him that sent Him. He was baptized of John, witnessed to by the Holy Spirit, and acknowledged by the Father to be a beloved Son.

". . . In the beginning the Gospel was to be preached, and . . . then faith came by hearing, and . . . baptism was to follow upon faith. . . .

"This then is the Word and will of the Lord, that all who hear and believe the Word of God shall be baptized. . . . Thereby they profess their faith and declare that they will henceforth live not according to their own will, but according to the will of God. For the testimony of Jesus they are prepared to forsake their homes, possessions, lands, and lives, and to suffer hunger, affliction, oppression, persecution, the cross and death for the same; yes, they desire to bury the flesh with its lusts, and arise with Christ to newness of life."
　　　　—Menno, *CW*, 121, 122

Baptism symbolizes a change of life: "Baptism shall be given to all those who [repent] . . . and

27

[who] believe truly that their sins are taken away through Christ, and to all those who desire to walk in the resurrection of Jesus Christ and be buried with Him in death, so that they might rise with Him; to all those who with such an understanding themselves desire and request it. . . ."

—*Schleitheim Confession*, 10

Baptism symbolizes cleansing: "Scripture describes baptism for us as signifying that through faith and the blood of Christ our sins are washed away: to the one baptized that his inner self has been changed, and that he believes, both before and afterward. It signifies that one should be and is dead to sin, and walking in newness of life and spirit; also that he shall certainly be saved by the inward baptism [of the Holy Spirit by Christ]."

—Conrad Grebel, *Programmatic Letters*, 29-31

Christ's inner baptism saves us: "The holy apostle Peter . . . says that even baptism doth also now save us, not the putting away of the filth of the flesh, but the convenant of a good conscience with God by the resurrection of Jesus Christ. [See 1 Peter 3:21.]

"Here Peter teaches us how the inward baptism saves us, by which the inner man is washed, and not the outward baptism by which the flesh is washed. For only this inward baptism . . . is of value in the sight of God, while outward baptism follows as an evidence of obedience which is of faith. For if outward baptism could save without the inward, then the whole Scriptures which speak of the new man would be spoken to no purpose ... Oh, no, outward baptism avails nothing so long as we are not inwardly renewed, regenerated, and baptized with the heavenly fire and the Holy Spirit of God."

—Menno, *CW*, 124, 125

Baptism is for believers only: "Since infant baptism is not expressly commanded of God ... it cannot be acceptable to the Lord, and consequently no promise can follow. Therefore the reader should know that true Christians ought not to be governed ... by the opinions and traditions of men, but by the Word and ordinances of God. For we have but one Lord and Master of our conscience, Jesus Christ. ..."

—Menno, *CW*, 126

The Word of God alone is our guide: " ... We must not and may not have our eye on lords and princes, nor on doctors and teachers of schools, nor on the councils of the fathers, and customs of long-standing. For against God's Word, neither emperors nor kings, nor doctors, nor licentiates, nor councils, nor proscriptions matter. We dare not be bound by any person, power, wisdom, or times, but we must be governed by the plainly expressed commands of Christ and the pure doctrines and practices of His holy apostles. ..."

—Menno, *CW*, 129

Unbaptized infants and children are saved and in the church: "And even as Abraham and the children of Israel, the female as well as the male, were in covenant not through the sign but through the election, so also are our children in the covenant of God, even though unbaptized.

". . . To children the kingdom of heaven belongs, and they are under the promise of the grace of God through Christ . . . and therefore, we truly believe that they are saved, holy and pure, and pleasing to God, under the covenant and in His church. . . ."

—Menno, *CW*, 133

"And although infants have neither faith nor baptism, think not that they are therefore damned. Oh, no! they are saved; for we have the Lord's own promise of the kingdom of God; not through any elements, ceremonies, and external rites, but solely by grace through Christ Jesus. And therefore we do truly believe that they are in a state of grace, pleasing to God, pure, holy, heirs of God and of eternal life. Yes, on account of this promise all sincere Christian believers may assuredly rejoice and comfort themselves in the salvation of their children."

—Menno, *CW*, 135

". . . Little children and particularly those of Christian parentage have a peculiar promise which was given them of God without any ceremony, but out of pure and generous grace, through Christ Jesus our Lord, who says, Suffer little children, and forbid them not, to come unto me; for of such is the kingdom of heaven. Matt. 19:14; Mark 10:14; Luke 18:16. This promise makes glad and assures all the chosen saints of

God in regard to their children or infants. By it they are assured that the true word of our Lord Jesus Christ could never fail. Inasmuch as He has shown such great mercy toward the children ... that He took them up in His blessed arms, blessed them, laid His hands upon them, promised them the kingdom ... and has done no more with them; therefore ... parents have in their hearts a sure and firm faith in the grace of God ... namely, that they are children of the kingdom of grace, and of the promise of eternal life. ... They train them in the love of God ... until these children are able to hear the Word of God, to believe it, and to fulfill it in their works. This is the time and not until then, of whatever age they may be, that they should receive Christian baptism. . . ."

—Menno, *CW*, 280, 281

The Lord's Supper

Symbols are described in the Bible as the realities they point to: " ... The paschal lamb was called the Lord's *pesach*, that is passover. The sign stood for the reality, for the lamb was not the passover ... but only signified the passover. ... So in the Holy Supper the bread is called the body, and the wine the blood of the Lord: the sign signifies the reality. Not that it actually is the flesh and blood of Christ, for with that He ascended into heaven and sitteth at the right hand of His Father, immortal and unchangeable, in eternal majesty and glory; but it is an admonishing sign and memorial to the fact that Christ Jesus the Son of God has delivered us from the power of the devil, from the dominion of hell and eternal death, by the sinless sacrifice of His innocent flesh and blood, and has led us triumphantly into the kingdom of His grace—as He Himself says: 'This do in remembrance of me.' "   —Menno, *CW*, 143, 144

Observe the Supper as Christ started it: "It shall be observed often and much. It shall not be observed except in conformity with Christ's rule in Matthew 18 [:15-18], for then it would not be the Lord's Supper. For without Matthew 18 everyone runs after the outward, and that which is inward, namely, love, one lets go; and brethren and false brethren go to the Supper together and eat. . . ."   —Conrad Grebel, *Programmatic Letters*, 23

Observe the Supper often: "Forget not to assemble yourselves together, but give diligence that you constantly meet together, and be united in prayer for all men, and in breaking of bread."   —Michael Sattler, *MM*, 420

The Holy Supper reminds us of Christ: " . . . The bread of the Holy Supper admonishes us: first, as to the bread as the body of Christ which He sacrificed for us, and the cup of the blood of Christ which he shed in great love for the remission of our sins. In the second place, it admonishes us to unity, love, and peace, which must be among all true Christians according to the Spirit, doctrine, and example of Christ. . . . In the third place, it admonishes us to a true regeneration which is of God; to all righteousness, thanksgiving, peace, and joy in the Holy Spirit, to a blameless life."

—Menno, CW, 150

To partake of Christ's flesh and blood is to yield to Him in faith: "All then who are in Christ and with believing, penitent hearts, [who] trust in the pure sacrifice of the body and blood of Christ confess that it is the only cleansing and atonement for their sins, the only and eternal means of grace. These really eat the flesh, and really drink the true blood of Christ, not with their mouths, but believingly in the spirit. . . .

" . . . He cannot be masticated nor digested in the body of any man. This . . . Augustine plainly acknowledges, saying, 'Why do you make ready teeth and stomach? Merely believe, and you have "eaten" Him already!' "

—Menno, CW, 154, 155

The bread (loaf) symbolizes unity through love: "Just as natural bread is made of many grains, pulverized by the mill, kneaded with water, and baked by the heat of the fire, so is the church of Christ made up of true believers, broken in their hearts with the mill of the divine Word, baptized with the water of the Holy Spirit, and with the fire of pure, unfeigned love made into one body. . . . In all things, one toward another, long-suffering, friendly, peaceable, ever ready in true Christian love to serve one's neighbor in all things possible: by exhortation, by reproof, by comforting, by assisting, by counsel-

ing, with deed and with possessions, yes, with bitter and hard labor, with body and life, ready to forgive one another as Christ forgives and serves us with His Word, life, and death."
—Menno, *CW*, 145, 146

Believers celebrate the Lord's Supper with holy joy: "Oh, delightful assembly and Christian marriage feast. ... Here no carnal pleasures ... but the glorious and holy mysteries, by means of the visible signs of bread and wine, are represented to and sought by true believers.

"Oh, delightful assembly and Christian marriage feast ... [with] peace and unity among all the brethren. The joyous word of divine grace ... His glorious benefits, favor, love, service, tears, prayers, His cross and death, are set forth.

"Oh, delightful assembly and Christian marriage feast ... [where] are invited [those] who are born of God, true Christians who have buried their sins, and who walk with Christ in a new and godly life ... who crucify the flesh and are driven by the Holy Spirit ... and in their weakness willingly serve and obey [God]. ...

"Oh, delightful assembly and Christian marriage feast ... where hungry consciences are fed with the heavenly bread of the divine Word, with the wine of the Holy Spirit, and where the peaceful, joyous souls sing and play before the Lord."
—Menno, *CW*, 148

Foot washing with fellow believers celebrates cleansing and mutual love: Christ established this ceremony "for two reasons. First, He would

34

have us know that He Himself must cleanse us after the inner man, and that we must allow Him to wash away the sins which beset us . . . and all filthiness of the flesh and spirit . . . that we may become purer from day to day.

"The second reason why Jesus instituted the ordinance of footwashing is that we shall humble ourselves among one another . . . and that we hold our fellow-believers in the highest respect— for the reason that they are the saints of God, and members of the body of Jesus Christ, and that the Holy Spirit dwells in them. . . ."

—Dirk Philips, *Enchirdion*, 389

6

CHRIST'S DISCIPLES
LIVE IN LOVE

Genuine faith bears good fruit. "True evangelical faith is of such a nature that it cannot lie dor-
mant, but manifests itself in all righteousness and
works of love; it ... clothes the naked ... feeds
the hungry ... comforts the sorrowful ...
shelters the destitute ... returns good for evil
... seeks that which is lost ... binds up that
which is wounded. ... The persecution, suffering, and anguish which befalls it for the sake of
the truth of the Lord is to it a glorious joy and
consolation."

—Menno, *CW*, 307

True Christians love God and neighbor. "There is nothing under heaven [the pious] love more than their God ... as they plainly testify and demonstrate by their actions. ... How can there ever be a greater love for God, and how can there be a more praiseworthy confession, than that one should be willing and ready not only to give up his temporal goods, ease, honor, and prosperity, but also to shun his dearest friend upon earth ... out of sincere regard for Christ, in obedience?" —Menno, *CW*, 973

"The Chief Emperor Christ has issued a decree, which decree He has sealed with His blood. In this directive it reads that we must be born again, must repent, deny ourselves, take up our cross, believe in Jesus Christ, and on this faith be baptized in the name of the Father, and the Son, and the Holy Spirit; must obey His commandments, give unto Caesar the things that are Caesar's; and love the Lord with all our heart and with all our strength, and our neighbor as ourselves. ..." —Menno, *CW*, 1024

Make Christ Lord of life. "Do not excuse yourselves, dear sirs and judges, because you are the servants of the emperor. ... It did not help Pilate that he crucified Christ in the name of the emperor. Serve the emperor in imperial matters, so far as Scripture permits, and serve God in divine matters. ...

"Do not usurp the judgment and kingdom of Christ, for He alone is the ruler of the conscience.

... Let Him be your emperor ... and His holy Word your edict, and you will soon have enough of storming and slaying. You must hearken to God above the emperor, and obey God's Word more than that of the emperor. ..."
—Menno, *CW*, 204

" ... True Christians ought not to be governed ... by the traditions of men, but by the Word and ordinances of God. For we have but one Lord and Master of our conscience, Jesus Christ. ..."
—Menno, *CW*, 126

Beware of cheap grace taught by some. "They preach nothing but the grace, the favor, the mercy, and the love of God before their covetous, proud, showy, impure, drunken, and impenitent church, little realizing that the whole Scriptures testify that such folk cannot inherit the kingdom of God. They strengthen the hands of the wicked so that no one repents of his wickedness—as the prophet complains."
—Menno, *CW*, 167

Avoid half-truths, as sometimes found in the state churches. " ... We know that you have demolished some of the little idols of Babylon, such as indulgences, invocation of deceased saints, unclean 'sanctity' [compulsory celibacy], distinctions regarding food, and the like, self-righteousness, idolatry, and other superstitions. But alas, the fearful blasphemy and abominations are retained, such as accursed unbelief, stiff-necked obstinacy, earthly-mindedness, unscriptural in-

fant baptism, the idolatrous [Lord's] Supper, and
the impenitent life. ..."

—Menno, *CW*, 168

Strive for holiness through Christ's Spirit.
"Those who are born from above are fearful of all
sin. They know by the Law that all which is
contrary to the original righteousness is sin, be it
inward or outward, important or trifling.
Therefore they fight daily with their weak flesh
in the Spirit and in faith. ... They approach the
throne of grace daily with contrite hearts and
pray, 'Holy Father, forgive us our trespasses as
we forgive those that trespass against us.' They
are not rejected by the Lord on account of such
lapses ... committed ... contrary to their will
... —for they are under grace. ... The seed of
God, faith in Christ Jesus, the birth which is of
God, and the anointing of the Holy Spirit remain
in them. ... They crucify their lusts as long as
they live; they watch and pray incessantly; and
although they are such poor, imperfect children,
they nevertheless rejoice in the sure trust of the
merits of Christ, and praise the Father for His
grace." —Menno, *CW*, 564

Scripture calls for total Christlikeness. "Although thou art pure, make thyself purer still; although thou art holy, make thyself holier still; although thou art righteous, make thyself more
righteous still. Adorn thyself with the white
silken robe of righteousness; hang about thy neck
the golden chain of every piety; gird thyself with
the fair girdle of brotherly love; put on the wed-

ding ring of a true faith; cover thyself with the precious fair gold of the divine Word; beautify thyself with the pearls of many virtues; wash thyself with the clear waters of grace, and anoint thyself with the oil of the Holy Spirit; wash thy feet in the clear, sparkling flood of Almighty God. . . . So will He desire thy beauty and will praise thee and say: How fair is thy love, my sister, my spouse!"

—Menno, CW, 221

Victory in Christ, not defeatism! The state churchmen "teach contrary to Paul (Romans 6) that one cannot be free of sin and live in righteousness. 'One must sin to the grave; no one can keep the commandments of God' (1 John 3, 5)—which is not true! The apostle of God [Peter] testifies, Christ bore our sins on his back that we might be without sin and live in righteousness. How can the priests dare to say that no one can do the right and not live without sin? (John 1, 1 Peter 2, 3): Christ took away our sin and undid the work of the devil . . . as Paul testified in Hebrews 2 that Christ took away the power of the devil, who had the power of death, so that He might deliver us who all our life had been in the fear of death and in bondage to slavery, that is, sin. As it stands in Titus 2: He delivered us from all kinds of unrighteousness. . . .

"The right done from the fear of God is acceptable to God."

—Martin Lingg (or Weninger),
called Lingki, "Vindication,"
MQR (Jl 1948, 183)

Victory over sin and Satan fulfills Genesis 3:15.
"To whomever this seed or Spirit is given, in him
the Spirit crushes the head of the serpent (Rom.
16)."

—Pilgram Marpeck, *Writings*, 61

*New life is possible because Christ transforms
us.* "The regenerate, therefore, lead a penitent
and new life, for they are renewed in Christ and
have received a new heart and spirit. Once they
were earthly-minded, now heavenly; once they
were carnal, now spiritual; once they were
unrighteous, now righteous; once they were evil,
now good; and they live no longer after the old
corrupted nature of the first earthly Adam, but
after the new upright nature of the new and
heavenly Adam, Christ Jesus. Even as Paul says:
'Nevertheless I live; yet not I, but Christ liveth in
me.' Their poor, weak life they daily renew more
and more, and that after the image of Him who
created them. Their minds are like the mind of
Christ; they gladly walk as He walked; they crucify and tame their flesh with all its evil lusts."

—Menno, *CW*, 93

Shun pomp and finery. "This kingdom is not a
kingdom in which they parade in gold, silver,
pearls, silk, velvet, and costly finery, as is done by
the haughty, proud world. ... But in the
kingdom of all humility (I declare) not the outward adorning of the body, but the inward
adorning of the spirit with zeal and diligence,
with a broken and contrite heart."

—Menno, *CW*, 217

Choose life, not death. " . . . Seek instruction, so that you may be taught and know which is the true way; for you may now choose life or death, good or evil; whichever you desire shall be given you. . . . If you delight in evil, so that you choose the pleasures of the world . . . lying and cheating, gambling, playing [cards], swearing, cursing, backbiting, hatred, envy, drunkenness, banqueting [orgies], excess, idolatry, covetousness, lasciviousness, vanity, filthy conversation, dancing, and so forth—which things, though the world does not consider them sins, but amusements, are nevertheless abominations in the eyes of the Lord. . . ."

—Soetgen van den Houte [1560 martyr] *MM*, 648a

Rely on Christ's Spirit. " . . . See that you adorn yourself with good works, namely, the works of the Spirit . . . goodness, gentleness, meekness, humility, obedience, long-suffering, righteousness, modesty, honorableness, purity, peaceableness, steadfastness, mercifulness, wisdom . . . good works, faith, hope, and love; to love God above all that is in the world, and to do to your neighbor as you would have men do unto you. . . ." —Soutgen van den Houte, *MM*, 649b

God watches over us. "I do not esteem my life more than the beloved men of God did theirs. Only perishable and mortal flesh which must sometime die can be taken from me, a flesh made to return to dust even though I should live half

the days of Methuselah. Not a hair can fall from my head without the will of my heavenly Father."
—Menno, *CW*, 194

"Elijah and Elisha, David, Daniel, Shadrach, Meshach, and Abednego, Peter, and Paul have all escaped the hands of the tyrant and none could injure a single hair on their head so long as the appointed day and hour were not come. So long as the Lord has more pleasure in our life than in our death they cannot injure us. . . ."
—Menno, *CW*, 1039

Though we suffer now, victory in Christ is certain. " . . . Quote all the councils, authors, and learned teachers there have been for centuries. Appeal to every lord and prince, every emperor, king, and mighty one on the earth. Use all the force, power, art, and cunning there is; it will avail you nothing. The Lamb will conquer and gain the victory; the people of God will triumph, not with external weapons but in patience, with the Spirit and Word of God. . . ."
—Menno, *CW*, 174

"Let them boast and rave, twist and wrangle, extirpate, persecute, and kill as they please. The Word will triumph and the Lamb will gain the victory. . . ."
—Menno, *CW*, 81

Walking with Christ brings us the wisdom of God. "Therefore be not intent upon the usages and customs of the fathers, nor upon the worldly wise and the learned ones. . . . For the wisdom of God which we teach is a wisdom which none may understand except those who are desirous of living and walking according to the will of God. It is that wisdom which is not to be brought from afar nor taught in schools of higher learning. It must be given from above and be learned through the Holy Spirit." —Menno, *CW*, 106, 107

Forgiveness is ours through Christ. "There was no forgiveness nor consolation of grace to be had unless the eternal Word, God's eternal Son, should come from high heaven, become man, [and] suffer hunger, temptation, misery, torture, the cross, and death, as the Scriptures teach."
—Menno, *CW*, 113

The gospel of Christ gives us comfort and hope. "Since it is plain from all these Scriptures that we must all confess ourselves to be sinners, as we are in fact; and since no one under heaven has perfectly fulfilled the righteousness required of God but Christ Jesus alone; therefore none can approach God, obtain grace, and be saved, except by the perfect righteousness, atonement, and intercession of Jesus Christ; however godly, righteous, holy, and unblamable he may be. We must all acknowledge, whoever we are, that we are sinners in thought, word, and deed. Yes, if we did not have before us the righteous Christ Jesus, no prophet nor apostle could be saved.

"Therefore be of good cheer and comforted in the Lord. You can expect no greater righteousness in yourself than all the chosen of God had in them from the beginning. In and by yourself you are a poor sinner, and by the eternal righteousness banished, accursed, and condemned to eternal death. But in and through Christ you are justified and pleasing unto God, and adopted by Him in eternal grace as a daughter and child. In this all saints have comforted themselves, have trusted in Christ, have ever esteemed their own righteousness as unclean, weak, and imperfect, have with contrite hearts approached the throne of grace in the name of Christ and with firm faith prayed the Father: O Father, forgive us our transgressions as we forgive those who trespass against us."   —Menno to Griet, wife of Rein Edes, *CW*, 1053

God's children are secure. " . . . The foundation on which the entire edifice of our faith must be placed is Christ Jesus alone. All who are built upon this ground will not be consumed by the fire of tribulation, for they are living stones in the temple of the Lord. They are like gold, silver, and precious stones and can never be made to collapse ("topple") by such gates of hell as false doctrine, flesh, blood, the world, sin, the devil, water, fire, sword, or by any other means, no matter how sorely they are tried. For they are founded on Christ, confirmed in the faith, and assured in the Word through the Holy Spirit so that they cannot be turned aside from the pure and wholesome doctrine of Christ by all the furious and bloody Neros under heaven, with all their cruel tyranny . . . for . . . [Christians] are as immovable as Mount Zion, like firm pillars, brave knights and pious, valiant witnesses of Christ. They have fought unto death and do so daily still (God be praised eternally). I speak of those who have the Spirit and Word of the Lord."

—Menno, *CW*, 329, 330

". . . Who shall separate us from the love of God? It can never be, if I am in the bonds of perfectness with Him, and love Him with a pure heart, a good conscience, and unfeigned faith, that anything could then turn me away or separate me from Him. For it is my only desire and highest joy to hear and speak of His Word, and in my weakness walk as He commanded and taught through His Son—let it cost money and possessions, flesh or blood, if that please Him."

—Menno, *CW*, 393

Marriage as a holy and lifelong covenant brings fulfillment. ". . . In this kingdom and under this King no other marriage is in effect save that between one man and one woman as God in the beginning ordained . . . and as Christ has once more formulated it that these two shall be one flesh, and that they shall not divorce except for the cause of adultery. Matt. 5:32."

—Menno, *CW*, 217

"These two, one husband and one wife, are one flesh and can not be separated from each other to marry again otherwise than for adultery, as our Lord says. Matt. 5:19; Mark 10; Luke 16."

—Menno, *CW*, 561

"I entreat all dear brethren . . . that they may act and walk in a becoming manner in the most holy covenant of grace before Him and all mankind, and live and walk with their life's partner in such piety, love, unity, and peace, and with such fidelity and care, that from now on we may [hear only] . . . of sincere Christian piety, of delight and godly joy."

—Menno, *CW*, 973

Share with the needy. "All those who are born of God, who are gifted with the Spirit of the Lord, who are . . . called into one body and love in Christ Jesus, are prepared by such love to serve their neighbors, not only with money and goods, but also after the example of their Lord . . . in an evangelical manner, with life and blood. They show mercy and love, as much as they can. No one among them is allowed to beg. They take to heart the needs of the saints. They entertain those in distress. They take the stranger into their houses. They comfort the afflicted; assist the needy; clothe the naked; feed the hungry; do not turn their face from the poor. . . . Isa. 58:7, 8."

—Menno, *CW*, 558

"Since we find that . . . [community of goods] was not permanent with the apostles . . . we . . . have never taught nor practiced community of goods. But we diligently and earnestly teach . . . assistance, love, and mercy. . . .

"And even if we did teach and practice community of goods . . . we would be but doing that

which the holy apostles full of the Holy Spirit did in the ... church at Jerusalem. ..."
—Menno, *CW*, 560

Live love and peace. "True believing Christians are sheep among wolves, sheep for the slaughter. They must be baptized in anxiety, distress, affliction, persecution, suffering, and death. They must pass through the probation of fire, and reach the Fatherland of eternal rest, not by slaying their bodily ... [enemies] but by mortifying their spiritual enemies. They employ neither worldly sword nor war, since with them killing is absolutely renounced."
—Conrad Grebel, *Programmatic Letters*, 29

"The sword is an ordering of God outside the perfection of Christ. It punishes and kills the wicked, and guards and protects the good. In the law [of Moses] the sword is established over the wicked for punishment and for death, and the secular rulers are established to wield the same.

"But within the perfection of Christ only the ban [excommunication] is used for the admonition and exclusion of the one who has sinned."
—*Schleitheim Confession*, 14

What about capital punishment? "If the transgressor should truly repent before his God and be reborn of Him, he would then also be a chosen saint and child of God, a fellow partaker of grace, a spiritual member of the Lord's body, sprinkled with His precious blood and anointed with His Holy Spirit ... and for such an one to be hanged on the gallows ... by another Christian ... would look somewhat strange and unbecoming. ...

"Again, if he remain impenitent, and his life be taken, one would unmercifully rob him of the time of repentance of which ... he might yet avail himself."

—Menno, *CW*, 920-1

Use only spiritual "weapons." "All who are moved by the Spirit of Christ know of no sword but the Word of the Lord. Their weapons are powerful: fervent prayer, a long-suffering and patient heart, strong, immovable faith, a living hope, and an unblamable life. ... With these the Gospel of the kingdom, the Word of peace, is to be propagated and protected against the gates of hell." —Menno, *CW*, 175

"If Christ fights His enemies with the sword of His mouth, if He smites the earth with the rod of His mouth, and slays the wicked with the breath of His lips; and if we are to be conformed unto His image, how can we then oppose our enemies with any other sword?"

—Menno, *CW*, 44

"It is true that God will punish Babylon, but not by His Christians."

—Menno, *CW*, 46

"Our weapons are not weapons with which cities and countries may be destroyed, walls and gates broken down, and human blood shed in torrents like water. But they are weapons with which the spiritual kingdom of the devil is destroyed and the wicked principle in man's soul is broken down, flinty hearts broken. . . ."

—Menno, *CW,* 198

Obey civil authorities when not contrary to God's Word. "We publicly and unequivocally confess that the office of a magistrate is ordained of God. . . . And moreover . . . we have obeyed them when not contrary to the Word of God. We intend to do so all our lives. For we . . . know what the Lord's Word commands in this respect. Taxes and tolls we pay as Christ has taught and Himself practiced. We pray for the Imperial Majesty, kings, lords, and princes, and all in authority. We honor and obey them."

—Menno, *CW,* 549

Church and state are separate kingdoms. "No external power has the right to rule, benefit, nor govern in Christ's kingdom."

—Pilgram Marpeck, *Writings,* 113

" . . . I conclude before my God that worldly power, for all its work, is not needed in the kingdom of Christ, whose kingdom is not of this world, and I further conclude that all who attempt to preserve the kingdom of Christ by stooping to the governing authority will be punished for it and come to shame. For our citizenship is in heaven."

—Pilgram Marpeck, *Writings,* 151

Affirm the truth and swear not at all. "It is . . . through fear of God [that] we do not swear, nor dare to swear. . . .

"It should be observed that Christ Jesus does not in the New Testament point His disciples to the Law in regard to the matter of swearing—the dispensation of imperfectness which allowed swearing—but He points us now from the Law to yea and nay, as to the dispensation of perfectness. . . . I (Christ) say unto you my disciples, 'Swear not at all. . . . But let your communication be yea, yea; nay, nay; for whatsoever is more than these cometh of evil.' Here you have Christ's own doctrine and ordinance concerning swearing." —Menno, *CW*, 518-9

OBEDIENCE TO
GOD'S WORD
BRINGS LIFE

Do not add to or take away from God's Word.
" . . . I dare not go higher nor lower, be more
stringent or lenient, than the Scriptures and the
Holy Spirit teach me; and that out of great fear
and anxiety of my conscience—lest I once more
burden the God-fearing hearts, who now have
renounced the commandments of men, with
more such commandments. Willfulness and
human opinions I roundly hate, and do not want
them. I know what tribulation and affliction they
. . . caused me for many years."
—Menno, CW, 484

Consider the context when interpreting. " . . . It is the nature of all heresies to tear a fragment from the Holy Scriptures. . . . [Unsound teachers] do not regard that which is written before or after, by which we may ascertain the right meaning. . . ."　　—Menno, *CW*, 268

Christ is the key to correct interpretation. "All Scripture both of the Old and New Testament rightly explained according to the intent of Christ Jesus and His holy apostles is profitable for doctrine, for reproof, for correction, for instruction in righteousness. 2 Tim. 3:16. But whatever is taught contrary to the Spirit and doctrine of Jesus is accursed of God. Gal. 1."
　　—Menno, *CW*, 312

Follow the Scriptures faithfully. "Let no one remove you from the foundation which is laid through the letter of the holy Scriptures, and is sealed with the blood of Christ and of many witnesses of Jesus." —Michael Sattler, *MM*, 419b

"The Scriptures cannot be broken, neither are we to take away from, or add to, the Word of God; nay, not even the smallest tittle or letter of the Gospel may be changed."
　　—Thomas von Imbroich, *MM*. 367

Live the clear teachings of the Bible. "The Word is plain and needs no interpretation: namely, 'Thou shalt love the Lord thy God with all thy heart, and with all thy soul, and with all thy strength, and thy neighbor as thyself.' Matt.

22:37, 39. Again, you shall give bread to the hungry and entertain the needy. Isa. 58:7. If you live according to the flesh you shall die, for to be carnally minded is death. The avaricious [who live for money], drunkards, and the proud shall not inherit the kingdom of God. God will condemn adulterers and fornicators. Rom. 8; 1 Cor. 6, and many like passages. All who do not understand such passages are . . . more like clods than Christians.''   —Menno, CW, 214

Choose to believe that Christ fulfilled the Old Testament law. ''If you want to appeal to the literal understanding and transactions of Moses and the prophets, then you must also become Jews, accept circumcision, possess the land of Canaan literally, erect the Jewish kingdom again, build the city and temple, and offer sacrifices and perform the ritual as required in the law. And you must declare that Christ the promised Saviour has not yet come, He who has changed the literal and sensuous . . . ceremonies into new, spiritual, and abiding realities.''
—Menno, CW, 217

Recognize that the entire Bible has authority for the church. ''We certainly hope no one of a rational mind will be so foolish a man as to deny that the whole Scriptures, both of the Old and New Testament, were written for our instruction, admonition, and correction, and that they are the true scepter and rule by which the Lord's kingdom, house, church, and congregation must be ruled and governed. Everything contrary to

Scripture, therefore, whether it be in doctrines, beliefs, sacraments, worship, or life, should be measured by this infallible rule and demolished by this just and divine scepter, and destroyed without any respect of persons."
—Menno, *CW*, 159, 160

Christians follow the more complete revelation of the New Testament. " . . . We must point out that now in the New Testament we are directed to the Spirit, Word, counsel, admonition, and usage of Christ. What these allow we are free to do, but what He forbids we are not free to do. To this all true Christians should conform, and not to doubtful histories and obscure passages from which we can draw nothing certain and which teach the very opposite of what the Lord's apostles publicly taught."
—Menno, *CW*, 186

Unsound teachers appeal to the Old Testament as if it were the final authority. " . . . The false prophets . . . embellish and disguise their deceptive doctrine with the old leaven of the letter as shadows and figures; for whatever of the New Testament they cannot defend they try to prove with the Old Testament and with the letter of the prophecies. From this fallacy many sects have come. . . ." —Dirk Philips, *Enchiridion*, 323

Some teachers misinterpret God's Word. " . . . Here you may notice how miserably . . . [Gellius Faber] twists the Word of the Lord. . . ."
—Menno, *CW*, 751

Depravity and pride of intellect stand opposed to God's Word. " . . . It is known to all true children of God who are enlightened by His Holy Spirit that human reason is in Adam so depraved through the bite of the old crooked serpent [the devil] that it has kept but little which is conducive to godliness. Yes, it has become so perverse, haughty, ignorant, and blind that it dares to alter, bend, break, gainsay, judge, and lord it over the Word of the Lord God. Nobody's spirit . . . yields. . . . Whereby the saving truth is often violated, and lovely peace and peaceful love made to endure much injury, infamy, and disgrace. . . ."

—Menno, *CW*, 961

The Word will be our judge. "Examine, I say, our doctrine, and you will find through the grace of God that it is the pure and unadulterated doctrine of Christ, the holy Word, the Word of eternal peace, the Word of eternal truth, the Word of divine grace, the Word of our salvation, the invincible Word, against which no gates of hell shall ever prevail; the two-edged sword that proceeds out of the mouth of the Lord, the sword of the Spirit by which all must be judged that dwell upon the earth."

—Menno, *CW*, 117

The church shall make central what God emphasizes. "Beloved in the Lord, I would here sincerely pray you that you would make a difference between commandment and commandment, and not consider all commandments as equally

weighty. For adultery, idolatry, shedding of blood, and the like shameful and abominable works of the flesh will be punished more severely than a misunderstanding in regard to the ban [excommunication], and particularly when not committed willfully and perversely. . . ."
—Menno, *CW*, 479

The church may trust the Holy Spirit to lead believers to the will of God. ". . . Those consciences that are . . . through the Scripture and the Holy Spirit free and unbound will freely and voluntarily, without the constraint of anyone, by the unction of the Holy Spirit, and not by pressure from men, do that which the Holy Spirit advises, teaches, and commands in the holy Scripture. . . ."
—Menno, *CW*, 479

Proclaim the Word. ". . . We preach, as much as possible, both by day and by night, in houses and in fields, in forests and wastes, hither and yon, at home or abroad, in prisons and in dungeons, in water and in fire, on the scaffold and on the wheel, before lords and princes, through mouth and pen, with possessions and blood, with life and death. We have done this these many years, and we are not ashamed of the Gospel of the glory of Christ. . . . For we feel His living fruit and moving power in our hearts, as may be seen in many places by the lovely patience and willing sacrifices of our faithful brethren and companions in Christ Jesus."
—Menno, *CW*, 633

Obey Christ's Great Commission. "Christ, after His resurrection, commanded His apostles saying, 'Go ye therefore, and teach all nations, baptizing them in the name of the Father, and of the Son, and of the Holy Spirit; teaching them to observe all things whatsoever I have commanded you; and lo, I am with you always, even unto the end of the world. Amen.' "

—Menno, *CW*, 120

" . . . We desire with ardent hearts, even at the cost of life and blood, that the holy Gospel of Jesus Christ and His apostles, which only is the true doctrine and will remain so until Jesus Christ comes again upon the clouds, may be taught and preached through all the world as the Lord Jesus Christ commanded His disciples as a last word to them while He was on earth. Matt. 28:19; Mark 16:15." —Menno, *CW*, 303

" . . . Jesus Christ sent His disciples to preach the Gospel to all people, to Gentiles as well as Jews. . . ." —Menno, *CW*, 676

Baptize those who believe. Some state churchmen challenged Menno to prove that baptism is a command. "I pointed them to the sixteenth chapter of Mark, where the Lord speaks, 'Go ye into all the world, and preach the Gospel to every creature. He that believeth, and is baptized shall be saved.' . . . Then I referred them to the twenty-eighth chapter of Matthew, where the Lord says, 'Go ye therefore and teach all nations,' or as the [Greek] text has it, 'Make all nations disciples and baptize them ... in the name of the Father, and the Son, and the Holy Spirit.' Neither did this satisfy them, for we read, said they, *baptizing,* and not *baptize them,* alhough, alas, they knew very well that the surest text, namely, the ... [Greek], has this in the imperative mood, *and baptize them*—a thing which I had not until then noticed. ...."

—Menno, *CW,* 682

Be a humble servant of the Word. "Brethren, I tell you the truth. ... I am no Enoch, I am no Elias, I am not one who sees visions, I am no prophet who can teach and prophesy otherwise than what is written in the Word of God and understood in the Spirit. ... I do not doubt that the merciful Father will keep me in His Word so that I shall write or speak nothing but that which I can prove by Moses, the prophets, the ... [writers of the gospels], and other apostolic Scriptures ... explained in the true sense, Spirit, and intent of Christ."

—Menno, *CW,* 310

Be faithful until the end. " ... Continue faithful to the Lord unto death; for the crown is not at the beginning, nor in the middle, but at the end."

—Jerome Segers, *MM,* 507

CHRIST IS COMING AGAIN

Christ will raise the dead and judge the world.
" ... We would ... with our spiritual Noah,
Christ Jesus, enter into the new and spiritual ark,
which is His church, ever watching lest the del-
uge of the coming wrath of God overtake us
unexpectedly. ... Yes, we would sincerely watch
for the coming of the Lord. ... We would have
oil in our lamps. ..."
—Menno, *CW*, 345

"Christ Jesus preached, was crucified, died,
and was buried. He arose and ascended into
heaven and is seated at the right hand of the

Almighty Father. . . . From thence He will come to judge the sheep and the goats, the good and the evil, the living and the dead."
—Menno, *CW*, 428

"Watch and pray; the Day is at hand, and comes speedily when we must all stand before the impartial judgment seat of our God, who judges without respect of persons, and will reward everyone according to his works."
—Menno, *CW*, 833

Hymn of Discipleship

My God, where shall I [direct] my flight?
  Ah, help me on upon the way;
The foe surrounds both day and night
  And [glad] my soul would rend and slay.
    Lord, God, Thy Spirit give to me,
    Then on Thy ways I'll constant be,
    And, in Life's Book, eternally!
—Menno, *CW*, 1065

WORD LIST

Abomination—That which causes extreme disgust and hatred.

Admonish—To urge obedience, to express warning or disapproval to, especially in a gentle, earnest, or solicitous manner.

Atonement—The bringing together of God and man through the sacrificial death of Christ; making amends for sin.

Avarice—Excessive desire for wealth; greed.

Carnal—Given to crude bodily pleasure and appetites; not spiritual.

Celibacy—The state of not being married, especially for religious reasons.

Chastise—To punish, as by whipping; to censure severely.

Defraud—To cheat someone by deception or fraud.

Depravity—Quality or state of being morally evil and sinful.

Desert—Deserved reward or punishment.

Diligence—Steady, earnest giving of oneself to an effort or action.

Discernment—Understanding of a thing; ability to know something that was hidden before.

Dispensation—A system of revealed commands and promises regulating human affairs.

Dissipation—Wasting one's resources foolishly, such as health or wealth.

Edict—An official, public command having the force of law.

Elect—Chosen for salvation through divine mercy.

Embellish—To make beautiful; to decorate.

Expound—Set forth, explain.

Extirpate—To pull by the root, to destroy completely.

Fallacy—A false idea, deceptive appearance.

Flinty—Unyielding, stern.

Formulated—Stated or expressed in a well-thought-out way.

Fornication—Human sexual intercourse other than between a man and his wife.

Gallows—A frame of upright posts and crossbeam for hanging criminals.

Heinously—Hatefully or shockingly evil.

Heresies—Religious opinions contrary to accepted church teachings.

Hypocrisy—Pretending to be what one is not; acting a lie.

Immortal—Free from death.

Impenitent—Not sorry for sin or wrong conduct.

Incessantly—Without interruption; continuously.

Incitement—Urge; spur.

Incomprehensible—That which cannot be fully understood.

Indulgence—An attempt by the church of the Middle Ages to cancel the punishment one was scheduled to suffer after death. Indulgences were even sold by the church, and supposedly granted one permission to sin without suffering for it later in purgatory.

Ineffable—Not able to be expressed in words.

Infallible—Unerring; incapable of error.

Intercessor—One who prays, petitions, or entreats in favor of another.

Invincible—Not able to be conquered, overcome, or subdued.

Invocation—A petition or prayer for help or support.

Justification—Right or just standing with God.

Knead—To work or press into a mass as with the hands.

Lament—Regret strongly.

Lasciviousness—Lewd, lustful attitude.

Lenient—Soft; mild or tolerant in disposition.

Licentiates—Persons having a license or degree to practice a profession, especially that of theology.

Lucre—Money, monetary gain.

Masticate—To chew; to grind and crush with the teeth in preparation for swallowing.

Mortifying—Putting to death; destroying the strength or functioning of.

Obstinacy–Stubbornness.

Omnipotent—Having unlimited authority and power.

Ordinances—A practice or ceremony decreed by deity or governing authority.

Orgies—Drunken revelry; excessive sexual indulgence, as at a wild party.

Paternal—Of or relating to a father.

Perverse—Turned away from what is right or good; corrupt.

Probation—Testing period to determine fitness.

Propagate—To pass along to offspring; to cause to continue or increase by reproduction.

Proscription—Restraint, restriction, or prohibition.

Pulverize—To crush, beat, or grind to very small pieces.

Putrid—Rotten; of bad odor; morally corrupt.

Regeneration—Spiritual renewal.

Renounce—To give up and refuse to do, usually by formal declaration.

Sanctification—Setting apart for sacred purpose or God's use.

Sovereign—Having supreme power; unlimited in authority.

Stringent—Tight; constricted; marked by strictness of rule or standard; rigid.

Tangible—Capable of being perceived or seen, especially by sense of touch or sight.

Theologians—People trained in the study of God and His Word, and His relation to the world.

Tribulation—Distress or suffering resulting from oppression or persecution; a trying experience.

Tyrant—A ruler uncontrolled by law or constitution who exercises power oppressively or brutally.

Unadulterated—Pure; unmixed.

Unequivocally—In a manner leaving no doubt; clearly.

Unfathomable—Not measurable; beyond human comprehension or grasp.

Unpremeditated—Not thought out before a thing is done.

Usurp—To seize by force and hold without right.

Usury—The lending of money with an interest charge for its use.

SOURCES QUOTED

Martyrs Mirror by T. J. van Braght (Scottdale, Pa.,
1938). Graphic descriptions of the martyrs and their
testimonies, with heavy emphasis on the Anabaptists of the sixteenth century.

Selected Writings of Hans Denck, edited by Edward
J. Furcha with Ford Lewis Battles, Pittsburgh, Pa.:
The Pickwick Press (Pittsburgh Original Text and
Translation Series, 1), 1976. Used by permission.

*Enchiridion or Hand Book of the Christian Doctrine
and Religion*, by D. Philips. Elkhart, Ind.: Mennonite Publishing Co., 1910.

Conrad Grebel's Programmatic Letters of 1524,
transcribed and translated by J. C. Wenger, Scottdale, Pa.: Herald Press, 1970.

"Martin Weninger's Vindication of Anabaptism,"
The Mennonite Quarterly Review, Goshen College,
Goshen, Ind. (Jl. 1948, 180-87).

Complete Writings of Menno Simons, Verduin-
Wenger. Scottdale, Pa.: Herald Press, Fourth Print-
ing, 1978.

Writings of Pilgram Marpeck, translated and edited
by William Klassen and Walter Klaassen.
Kitchener, Ont., and Scottdale, Pa.: Herald Press,
1978.

Schleitheim Confession, translated and edited by John
H. Yoder. Scottdale, Pa., and Kitchener, Ont.:
Herald Press, 1977.

J.C. Wenger is professor of Historical Theology in Goshen Biblical Seminary, a school of the Associated Mennonite Biblical Seminaries, Elkhart, Indiana. He has made a lifelong study of Anabaptism and has published numerous articles and books in the field.

He studied at Eastern Mennonite and Goshen Colleges (BA), at Westminster and Princeton Theological seminaries, and at the universities of Basel, Chicago, Michigan (MA in Philosophy), and Zurich (ThD).

He has taught at Eastern Mennonite and at Union Biblical (India) seminaries, and has served on the Committee on Bible Translation, which prepared the *New International Bible*.

He is a member of the Evangelical Theological Society. He has served on the editorial boards of the

Mennonite Quarterly Review, of *Studies in Anabaptist and Mennonite History,* and of the *Mennonite Encyclopedia,* and on the executive council of the Institute of Mennonite Studies.

He has served the Mennonites as a deacon, a minister, and a bishop. He has been a member of their Historical Committee, Publication Board, Board of Education, district and general conference executive committees, and of the Presidium of the Mennonite World Conference.

He married the former Ruth D. Detweiler, RN, in 1937. They are the parents of two sons and two daughters.

A familiar sight in his home city of Goshen is J. C. riding his bicycle on a local errand.